Lean Simplified

The Power Laws of Speed

Jay Arthur

Published by LifeStar
2244 S. Olive St.
Denver, CO 80224-2518
(888) 468-1535 or (303) 281-9063 (orders only)
(888) 468-1537 or (303) 756-9144 (phone)
(888) 468-1536 or (303) 753-9675 (fax)
lifestar@rmi.net
www.qimacros.com

Upgrade Your KnowWare®!

Any Lean Six Sigma Book can be customized to reflect a company's improvement process. For information, call, write, or e-mail to the address above.

Also by Jay Arthur:
Lean Six Sigma DeMYSTiFieD, A Self Teaching Guide, McGraw Hill, 2006
Six Sigma Simplified (3rd), Breakthrough Improvement Made Easy, LifeStar, 2004
The Six Sigma Instructor's Guide (2nd), Greenbelt Training Made Easy, LifeStar, 2003
The Small Business Guerrilla Guide to Six Sigma ,LifeStar, 2003

Phone, Fax, or E-mail support: Contact Lifestar at the phone, fax or e-mail address above for any questions you have about Six Sigma or using this book.

On-site Workshops:

- **Lean Six Sigma Simplified One-Day:** qimacros.com/orderseminr.html
- **Lean Six Sigma for Healthcare One-Day:** qimacros.com/leansixsigmahealthcare.html
- **Lean for Healthcare Labs Two-Days:** qimacros.com/lean-lab-workshop.html
- **SPC Simplified One Day:** qimacros.com/pdf/spcworkshop/pdf

Free downloads available from www.qimacros.com/freestuff.html

- Lean Six Sigma SPC 30-day Evaluation Software for Excel
- QI Macros User Guide (1Mb PDF)
- Free Ebooks and Quick Reference Cards
- Free Lean, Six Sigma and QI Macros Articles

Table of Contents

You must change the wiring in your mind from make-and-sell (which has been deeply imprinted into your thinking) to a different mode—sense-and-respond. It requires shifting from a product-centric to a customer-centric way of looking at things.
Stephan Haeckel
Adaptive Enterprise

3

Lean Simplified
The Fast Eat The Slow!

Being fast has less to do with working longer or harder than with the things you stop doing and how you remove speed bumps!
- Jason Jennings and Lawrence Haughton

The Economies of Speed

Increasingly unpredictable and rapid change follows unavoidably from doing business in an Information Age. The only kind of strategy that makes sense in the face of unpredictable change is a strategy to become adaptive.
Stephan Haeckel
Adaptive Enterprise

Customers today demand speed and customized solutions. I don't know about you, but I grew up on the wisdom of Henry Ford: mass production and the *economies of scale*. But while I was learning about Ford in the 50's, Toyota was mastering the art of *lean production* and the *economies of speed*.

Speed is not Haste

You don't have to work harder or faster to gain more speed. Speed involves removing every speed bump, barrier, and obstacle from your path. It also involves shedding excess weight along the way.

Slow is not a virtue

Slow people believe that their businesses are unique. Their products may be unique, but the processes used to create them are not. Every business process suffers from two unwanted by-products:

- **Defects**
- **Delay** which has three components:
  1. The time to complete large batches of product
  2. Rework of defects
  3. Decision making

The only thing that cannot be converted to lean and quick changeover is corporate culture. It took Toyota 35 years; you will not do it overnight.

The Power Laws of Speed

When you shorten lead times and focus on keeping production lines easily changeable, you actually get higher quality, faster response times, better productivity and better use of equipment and space.

At the end of 2003, Toyota's annual profit, at $8.3 Billion, was larger than GM, Chrysler, and Ford combined.

Typical results from implementing lean thinking:

- 90% reduction in lead times
- 90% reduction in all inventories
- 100% increase in productivity
- 50% reduction in errors
- Fewer injuries

The 5% Rule

The actual time required to produce a product or deliver a service is *only 5 percent of the total elapsed time.*

The 25-2-20 Rule

Every 25 percent reduction in elapsed time will *double productivity and reduce costs by 20 percent.*

The 3X2 Rule

Companies that routinely reduce the elapsed time to deliver enjoy *growth rates three times the average with twice the profit margins.*

Customers will pay a premium for speed.

Inshoring Oddly enough, when you go lean, you no longer need to offshore work which, by design, requires large inventories be shipped for weeks over oceans and then transported from ports on the coast.

Economic Bounce About half of the downswing in any economy is caused by companies and customers working off finished inventories that were built up earlier by mass production. In a lean economy, there are no inventories to work off.

The Origins of Lean

Lean thinking originated at Toyota with the Toyota Production System (TPS). The original ideas were formulated by Sakichi Toyoda in the 1920s and 1930s. Taiichi Ohno began to implement these ideas in the 1940s but only made the leap to full implementation in the 1950s.

Many of the principles of lean came from a surprising source: American supermarkets where small quantities of a vast selection of inventory is replenished as customers "pull" them off the shelf. This is the kanban system.

The hardest part of learning to think lean is abandoning old ideas about economies of scale and mass production. These are basically "push" systems based on *projected* customer demand. Quality is "inspected" into the product. These "batch-and-queue," push system ideas must be the first casualties of the lean transformation.

In lean, quality, productivity and low cost come from producing small batches (ideally one) of a given product, start-to-finish without any piles of partially finished goods.

The principles of lean are pretty simple, whether you apply them to manufacturing, service, or administration.

Core Ideas

1. **Determine and create value**—what does the customer want?

2. **Use "pull" instead of "push" systems** to avoid overproduction. Inventories hide problems and inefficiencies.

3. **One piece flow**—Make the work "flow," so that there are no interruptions and no wasted time or materials.

4. **Eliminate the seven speed bumps caused by waste** using the five S's—sort, straighten, shine, standardize, and sustain.

5. **Use the "five whys?" and Six Sigma problem solving** to eliminate defects.

The Origins of Lean

- Lead-time by 46%
- WIP inventory, 83%
- Finished goods inventory, 91%
- Overtime, 50%
- And increased productivity by 83%.

(Source: The Toyota Way, Jeffrey Liker)

What's weird about this kind of thinking?

1. Sometimes the best thing you can do is to **stop making stuff.** Unused inventory is waste.
2. The top priority is to produce products at the rate of customer demand, not keeping workers busy.
3. It's usually best to work out a process manually first before adding technology.
4. Create a small inventory of finished goods to level out the production schedule.
5. The more inventory you have, the less likely you will have what you need!

Lean vs Mass Production

The old models of business required stability, not the unpredictable nature of today's markets. In the good old days, you could make and sell products using some sort of strategic planning. In the volatile, ever-changing marketplace of today, however, you must be able to rapidly sense what customers want and respond to their needs quickly.

Lean Production	Mass Production
Build to Order	Make and Sell
Economies of Speed	Economies of Scale
Effective	Efficient
Pull (from Customer)	Push (to customer)
Small Lots	Large Batches
Quick changeover	Changeover unimportant
Production Cells	Functional Silos
Right-sized Machines	Big, Fast Machines Interchangeable parts
Fast to respond	Slow to change
Adaptive	Rigid, inflexible
General knowledge	Specialized knowledge

You Already Understand Lean

Lean Kitchens

Kitchens have long been designed as "cells" for food preparation. The refrigerator, sink and stove should form a "V". My kitchen looks like this:

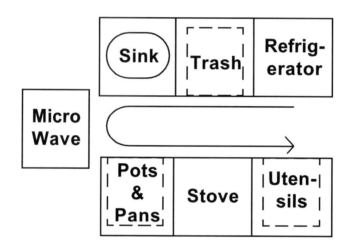

Food comes out of the refrigerator, gets washed in the sink, cut up on the counter, cooked on the stove, and delivered to the table. Unlike mass production where different silos would be put in charge of frozen and refrigerated food, washing, cutting and cooking, there's usually only one cook that handles each of these steps. Each meal is a small "lot". We never cook in batches big enough for the entire week. Limited inventories of raw materials are replenished by a trip to the supermarket.

The Fast Food Experience

If you walk into a Subway, your sandwich is created right in front of you and it's ready when you pay. In contrast, have you ever been to a restaurant where you place your order, pay and then stand in a crowd of other people waiting for their sandwich? The crowd forms right in front of the soda machine and the door to the bathroom creating bottlenecks.

Lean Management

In the Organized Executive, Stephanie Winston suggests that the best way to handle anything that crosses your desk is to TRAF it: toss it, refer it, act on it or file it. This is the essence of lean thinking and one piece flow.

Creating Value

The starting point for implementing lean is the concept of *value* and the *value stream*. Value is defined by the customer, not the company, business unit, manager, or employee. When I worked in information technologies, for example, programmers often focused on cool, new technology, not on what was fast, proven and effective for the customer. Craftsmen bear allegiance to their craft, not to their customer.

Since most businesses have grouped work together into functional silos, the definition of value is often skewed by each silo. While each silo attempts to optimize its own operation, tremendous waste is created by failing to optimize the overall flow of products and services.

Value Streams

The value stream includes every activity required to deliver a product or service. Sadly, only about 5 percent of any non-lean process adds value; 95 percent is non-value added effort and delay—what Toyota calls *muda* (waste).

Most people find this hard to believe, but when you take the perspective of the product or service and notice how long you sit around waiting for something to happen, how many things go wrong and have to be reworked, you get some idea of the waste in the process.

All of this delay and rework can be eliminated using Lean and Six Sigma.

The goal is to line up all of the essential steps into a continuous flow with no wasted motions, interruptions, batches or queues. When you do, **the amount of people, time, technology, space, and inventories required can be cut in half.**

To do this, start by listening to the voice of the customer and evaluating how all of your activities support their needs. The Lean Six Sigma tool for doing this is called the Voice of the Customer matrix.

Establish the Voice of the Customer

Gather the customer's needs and wants as a basis for establishing objectives.

Why?

When?

Before taking action to reorganize the work flow.

How?

1 Enter key customer voice statements on left. Rate the importance from 1 (low) to 5 (high).

2 Identify and enter key business functions along the top.

3. For each center box, rate the "how" (top) to the "what" (left). Multiply times the importance to get the total weight.

4. Highest scores show where to focus your improvement efforts.

Sense-and-respond does not always mean listen-and-comply.
Stephan Haeckel
Adaptive Enterprise

(QI Macros VOC.xlt template for Excel)

The Seven Speed Bumps of Lean

The Seven Mudas

Case Study

In 2004, GM announced reduced production for 2005 because of unsold inventories of 2004 cars and trucks.

Muda—**non-value added waste**—is any activity which absorbs money, time, and people but creates no value.

1. **Over production** (the most common type of waste) which creates inventories that take up space and capital.
2. **Excess inventory** caused by over production.
3. **Waiting**—Don't you hate standing in line? So do your products or services. Are they always waiting for the next value-adding process to start?

   Don't you hate waiting on your computer to boot up? So do employees. Are they waiting for missing parts or late meeting attendees?
4. **Unnecessary movement** of work products. When you break down the silos into cells, the work products don't have to travel so far between processes.
5. **Unnecessary movement** of employees. Are parts and tools too far from where they're needed? (Have employees wear pedometers to measure daily travel. You'll be surprised by the miles they travel in non-lean workspace.)
6. **Unnecessary or incorrect processing.** Why have people watch a machine that can be taught to monitor itself?
7. **Defects** leading to repair, rework, or scrap.

Lean thinking will help you reduce or eliminate numbers 1-5. Six Sigma will help you reduce 6 and 7.

When you rearrange your production floor into production cells with right-sized machines and quick change over, **you can quickly reduce most of these common kinds of waste by 50-90 percent.**

The simplest way to begin to move toward lean is to flowchart the value stream and analyze each element for non-value added work. Then redesign the flow to eliminate as much of the non-value added work as possible and standardize the ongoing process.

The Antidote to Waste

The Five S's

Case Study

I worked with one hospital lab. In a lab of 2,400 sq. ft. the team threw out two dumpsters of unused and out of date equipment and supplies.

To remove the waste, we turn to the five S's. The principles of reorganizing work so that it's simpler, more straightforward, and visually manageable are:

1. **Sort** — keep only what is needed. Pitch everything else. The workplace often becomes cluttered with products, tools, and waste materials that don't really belong there. Get rid of them.
   - Sort through everything in the target area: What is it for? Why do we have it? How often is it used?
   - Remove or Red Tag: unnecessary material or unnecessary equipment
   - During the sort, move all items to appropriate holding place

2. **Straighten** — A place for everything and everything in its place. Establish standardized places for incoming raw materials, tools, etc.
   - Determine the location for needed items: move higher usage items closer to the user; put information and tools at "arms length."
   - Make it obvious where things belong: labels, signboards, maps, and outlines or shadows.

3. **Shine** — clean machines and work area to expose problems.
   - Determine what needs to be cleaned.
   - Find proper cleaning equipment (5S tool kit).
   - Establish cleaning schedule.
   - Define responsibility for common areas.

4. **Standardize** — develop systems and procedures to monitor conformance to the first three rules. (This includes the define and measure aspects of Six Sigma's DMAIC.)

5. **Sustain** — maintain a stable workflow. (This includes the Analyze, Improve, and Control phases of Six Sigma.)

Pull vs Push

Case Study

Using "pull," Bumper Works reduced elapsed time from arrival of a flat sheet of steel to the shipment of a finished bumper from 28 to 2 days.

(Source:Lean Thinking, Womack & Jones)

When I was 14, my father taught me how to shoot trap. In trap or skeet shooting, you stand at a position, and load your Remington Wingmaster 20 gauge shotgun. After you shout "Pull", a clay target flies from the trap—left, right, or straight away. Then you do your best to break the target with a single shot.

Notice that nothing happens until you (the customer) "pull" the clay target from the trap. Compare this with mass production that produces large batches of finished inventory in anticipation of future demand.

I call this "Field of Dreams" thinking: *If you build it, they will come.* Unfortunately, customers increasingly want products customized to their needs delivered when they need it, not when you can deliver it.

What we need instead is "Field of Reality" thinking: *When they come, you will build it fast and right the first time.*

Instead of producing inventory for projected demand, *pull* thinking forces you to produce parts and products when the customer actually orders them. If a customer orders a car, for example, it should kick off a series of requests for a frame, doors, tires, engines, etc. which should kick off a series of requests for raw materials, and so on.

In Tokyo, for example, you can place a custom order for a Toyota and have it delivered within five days.

Pull means that no one produces anything until a customer asks for it, but when they do, you make it very quickly. This is accomplished by implementing one-piece flow.

Redesign For One Piece Flow

Benefits:

1. Builds in quality
2. Creates flexibility
3. Increases productivity
4. Frees flow and space
5. Improves safety
6. Improves morale
7. Reduces inventory

The trick is eliminating all of the delay between value-adding steps and lining up all of the machines and processes so that the product or service flows through the value channel without interruption. Mass production and large batches ensure that the product will have to sit patiently waiting for the next step in the process.

The mental shift required to move from mass production to lean thinking is to focus on continuous flow of small lots.

The Redesign Process

1. The first step is to focus on the part, product or service itself. Follow the product through its entire production cycle.

In a hospital you would follow a patient through from admission to discharge. In a printing company, you'd follow a job from start to delivery. In a manufacturing plant, you'd follow the product from order to delivery.

2. The second step is to ignore traditional boundaries, layouts, etc. In other words, forget what you know.

3. The third step is to realign the work flow into production "cells" to eliminate delay, rework, and scrap.

4. The fourth step is to "right size" the machines and technology to support smaller lots, quick changeover, and one-piece flow. This often means using simpler, slower, and less automated machines that may actually be more accurate and reliable.

The goal of flow is to eliminate all delays, interruptions and stoppages, and not to rest until you succeed.

Common measures of flow:

- Lead (or cycle) time: time product stays in the system
- Value-added ratio: (Value-added time)/(lead time)
- Travel distance of the product or people doing the work
- Productivity: (people hours)/unit
- Number of handoffs
- Quality rate or first pass yield

Spaghetti Diagrams

Why?

When?

To define existing flow before redesigning it.

How?

1. Use square Post-it™ notes to lay out floor plan of machines or processing stations.

2. Draw arrows to show movement of product or service through the floor plan

3. Assess how many times each processing station is used. Is the highest volume closest to incoming materials or products?

4. Identify ways to redesign the flow to reduce unnecessary movement of materials.

Define the <u>existing</u> processing layout as a basis for improvement.

Here's an example from a hospital laboratory. There are five main processing areas: hematology, chemistry, coag, urinary analysis (UA), and microbiology. Many of these areas have both automated analyzers and manual processes.

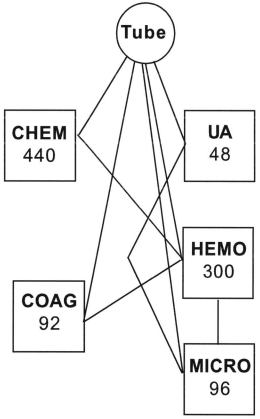

Notice that although HEMO has 300 orders a day, it's farther from the pneumatic tube than UA which only has 48. Moving HEMO and Micro closer to the tube and UA farther from the tube could reduce unnecessary travel of hundreds of samples.

Once redesigned, the hospital lab saved:

- 17% of floor space
- 54% of travel time
- 7 hours of delay per day

Cells vs Silos

Case Study

Wiremold reduced time-to-market by 75%, space by 50%, cycle time from 28 days to 2 days, and reduced defects by over 40% *per year.* Changeovers increased from four per day to 30 per day.

(Source:Lean Thinking, Womack & Jones)

In mass production, work is grouped by function into silos and completed batches of product pile up in-between.

In lean, production flow is organized in cells that handle the entire production process. A cell is a close, u-shaped arrangement of people and machines in a processing sequence to facilitate flow.

Direction of Flow

When you see diagrams from Toyota and other lean companies, flow goes counterclockwise. While I don't know if this is essential, it does help break up our normal modes of thinking.

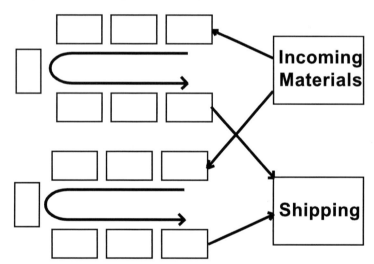

In the case of the hospital lab, we rearranged the automated blood processors into one work cell.

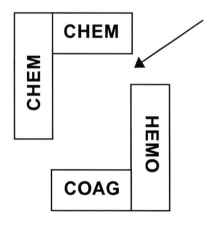

Map The Value Stream

Define the <u>existing</u> or improved process as a starting point for stabilization and improvement.

Why?

When?

To define existing flow before Value-Added Analysis or after improvement.

How?

1. Start with identifying customer needs and end with satisfying them.

2. Use square Post-it™ notes to lay out activities.

3. Use Arrow Post-its to show delays.

4. Place activities in the correct order.

5. Identify Inventory levels carried between each step.

Case Study

I worked with one goverment organization that had a process that took 140 days, but there was only 7.5 hours of real work in all 140 days. We reduced it to 30.

Value Stream Mapping symbols:

Process 1 CT = 15 sec Crew = 1 CO = 10 min Uptime = 100% Waste = 5% Available Sec = 27600	Process	Adding value to the product or service (verb–noun) CT = Cycle Time CO = Change Over Time Uptime = 0-100% Waste = 0-100% Available Seconds = 28,800 / 8 hr shift
△ 100 Units	Inventory	Amount of inventory carried between process steps
▷ 100 Secs	Arrow	Showing the flow and transition

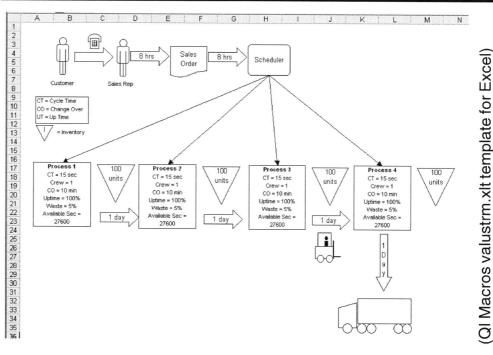

(QI Macros valustrm.xlt template for Excel)

Identify The Non-Value Added Elements

Why?

When?

To slash cycle time and double your speed.

How?

1. For each arrow, box, and diamond, list its function and the time spent.

2. Now become the customer's order and ask:
   - Is the order delayed?
   - Is this inspection necessary?
   - Does it "add value," or is this just waste or rework?

3. Most of the delay is in the arrows. How can delays be eliminated or shortened to accelerate your productivity?.

Identify the wait time, walk time, waste, rework, and delay that can be eliminated from the process.

	A	B	C	D	E
1		Value Added Checklist			
2	Activity, Decision, Arrow	Time Spent (hours, days, weeks, months)	Adds Value (not inspection or fix-it work)	Changes Product or Service Physically	Right The First Time (not waste or rework)
3	Claim Received	1 min	Y	Y	Y
4	Arrow to Establish Control	5 day	N	N	N
5	Establish Control	-	Y	Y	Y
6	Arrow to Create Folder	10 min	N	N	N
7	Create Folder	-	Y	Y	Y
8	Arrow to Need Evidence?	25 days	N	N	N
9	Need Evidence? (inspection/decision)	3 min	N	N	Y
10	No: Arrow to Exam Needed?	2 days	N	N	N
11	Yes: Arrow To Request Evidence	1 day	N	N	N
12	Request Evidence	45 min	Y	Y	Y
13	Arrow to Evidence Received? 90	60 days	N	N	N
14	Evidence Received? Days	-	N	N	Y
15	No: Arrow to Provide Letter	5-10 days	N	N	N
16	Yes: Arrow to Exam Needed?	2 days	N	N	N
17	Provide Letter	30 min	Y	Y	Y
18	Arrow to Exam Needed?	30 days	N	N	N
19	Exam Needed? (decision)	15 min	Y	Y	Y
20	No: Arrow to Rate Claim	-	N	N	N
21	Yes: Arrow to Request Exam	-	N	N	N
22	Request Exam	1 hour	Y	Y	Y
23	Arrow to Exam Complete? 36	-	N	N	N
24	Exam Complete? (decision) Days	25 days	N	N	Y
25	No: Arrow to Request Exam	-	N	N	N
26	Yes: Arrow to Rate Claim	90-100 days	N	N	N
27	Rate Claim	3 hours	Y	Y	Y
28	Arrow to Claims Review	1 day	N	N	N
29	Claims Review	2 days	N	N	Y
30	Arrow to Error Noted?	-	N	N	N
31	Error Noted? (Inspection/decision)	-	N	N	N
32	No: Arrow to Prepare Award	3-14 days	N	N	N
33	Yes: Arrow to Rate Claim (rework)120	1 day	N	N	N
34	Prepare Award Days	15 min	Y	Y	Y
35	Arrow to Rating Correction Needed?	-	N	N	N
36	Rating Correction Needed? (Decision)	-	N	N	Y
37	No: Arrow to Authorizer Review	2 days	N	N	N
38	Yes: Arrow to Rate Claim (rework)	-	N	N	N
39	Authorizer Review	8 min	N	N	Y
40	Arrow to Rating Correction Needed?	-	N	N	N
41	No: Arrow To Award Correction Needed?	-	N	N	N
42	Yes: Arrow to Rate Claim (rework)	-	N	N	N
43	Award Correction Needed?	-	N	N	Y
44	No: Arrow to Authorize Award	-	N	N	N
45	Yes: Arrow to Prepare Award (Rework)	-	N	N	N
46	Authorize Award	-	Y	Y	Y
47	Arrow to Mail Award Notice	-	Y	Y	Y

Standardized Work

The Sixth "S"

Case Study

I worked with one computer operations group that reduced nightly batch processing from 8 hours to 1 hour by letting the system handle analysis of return codes.

Standardized work consists of three elements: Takt time, sequence, and inventory.

1. Takt Time synchronizes the rate of production to the rate of sales. All production is organized around this key measurement. Think of *takt* time as a speedometer that measures the rate of production.

$$\text{Takt Time} = \frac{\text{Available hours worked per day}}{\text{Required production to meet demand}}$$

If, for example, the company sells 100 widgets per day and has an eight hour production shift, takt time would be:

(8 hrs * 60 min)/(100 widgets/day) = 4.8 min/widget

Higher production causes the *muda* (waste) of overproduction. Under production causes backorders.

In mass production most groups act like they are race cars trying to produce the most stuff, regardless of whether the next step in the process can use it. In lean production, groups act like train cars that move purposely together.

In one-piece-flow, every step in the process should be producing one widget within the takt time. Lean facilities use *andon* boards to display actual takt time to allow for immediate adjustments due to changes in sales.

Andon boards are like a car's dashboard that show speed (takt time) and warning lights to alert workers to problems.

2. Sequence of work processes — to minimize the seven types of waste using the five S's—sort, straighten, shine, standardize, and sustain.

3. Inventory on hand required to complete the product.

Leveling

Of course, once you understand the patterns of demand, you can start to level the production of your product or service. While there might be more cost associated with changeover from one product to the next, these can be minimized by producing small lots every day that mirror actual demand.

Lean Problem Solving

The Seventh "S"

There is another "S" in lean thinking: **Stop!**
Every person on the line has the right to stop production when an error is detected. Stopping production is far cheaper than producing defective parts that simply have to be fixed later.

When the line stops, there are visual signals (trouble lights) on the *andon* board that show exactly where the process stopped so that problem solving can begin immediately.

Production Floor Problem Solving

Your goal is to compete against perfection, not competitors. Here's where Six Sigma comes into play. The idea of *perfection through endless improvements*, is key to lean thinking. **You can't start at perfection, but you can arrive at perfection by iteration.**

Most problems do not call for complex statistical analysis. Instead, they need painstaking, detailed problem solving.

1. Go and see—go to where production was stopped.

2. Analyze the situation

3. Use one-piece flow and andon to surface problems

4. Ask "why?" five times

Six Sigma Problem Solving

Six Sigma can help drill down into more complex problems using data collected from daily operation.

Seeing and hearing things with your own eyes and ears is a critical first step in improving or creating a breakthrough. Once you start observing carefully, all kinds of insights and opportunities can open up.
Tom Kelly
CEO of IDEO

How is Lean different from Six Sigma?

Lean	Six Sigma
Productivity (Speed)	Quality (Good)
Eliminate non-value-added effort	Reduce defects
Analysis of flow	Analysis of defect data
Five S's	DFSS
Five Whys?	DMAIC

What to do?

Lean thinking will invariably free up cash, people, and space.

How do I get started?

The most difficult step is the first one. You will need a change agent, a crisis in a mission critical process (externally or internally generated), and a determination to get results quickly. Then you'll need the determination to keep going. Leaders and employees who thrive on change and continuous improvement are often in short supply.

Demand immediate results. Pick a pilot area that's open to change and jump right in. Line up the machines and work steps. Eliminate delays. Slash the inventories. Dramatic reductions in lead times, inventories, space, and defects should be possible in six to twelve months.

Stay the Course. It may take five years to fully integrate lean into your business.
- 3 years to get a lean system fully in place.
- 2 years to make it self-sustaining.

Develop a Scorecard

Develop a scorecard of key measures:

- Sales/employee (productivity)
- Products delivered on time (customer service)
- Inventory turns
- defects/million (quality)

Set BHAGs

Set big, hairy audacious goals (BHAG)

- 20% increase in sales per employee
- 50% reduction in defects every year
- 100% on-time delivery
- Reduce order-to-ship time to less than a day
- 20 Inventory turns per year
- Reduce time-to-market by 75%
- Reduce costs (hours/widget)

Next Steps

Case Study

Pratt and Whitney rightsized their turbine blade machines which increased actual processing time from 3 minutes to 12, but reduced total cycle time from 10 days to 75 minutes. Parts in process fell from 1,640 to 15. Space reduced by 60%. Total costs cut by 50%.

(Source:Lean Thinking, Womack & Jones)

Get Started Immediately

- Reorganize your company by product family and value stream. Topple the silos and implement flow.
- Move the machines and people into product cells immediately.
- Reduce the number of suppliers.
- Help your remaining suppliers implement "lean."
- Downsize the laggards.
- Two-steps forward and one-step back is okay.
- Devise a growth strategy.
- Kaizen (i.e., improve) each value stream multiple times.
- Teach Lean thinking and Six Sigma skills to each pilot project as you go.
- Right-size your machines and tools.

What can you do with all those people?

Lean will free up 30% of your staff. The traditional response of downsizing will only make everyone resistant to "lean" and improvement. So let me ask you this:

If you could add 30% more people at no cost, what unstarted projects or new lines of business would you pursue that you can't now because you don't have the resources?

What can you do if something goes wrong and sales fall off?

1. Reduce overtime and/or cut the work week.
2. Put people to work on improvement projects to save more cash.
3. Insource work from suppliers.
4. Develop new lines of business to grow revenues.

Glossary

Cell: a close arrangement of people and machines in a processing sequence to facilitate flow.

Kanban: Japanese word for card, ticket, or sign. It's a key tool for managing flow in a pull system. In a grocery store, it's the card at the back of the shelf indicating the product is sold out or back ordered.

Andon: Visual signal that alerts workers to problems. Andon is like a dashboard with warning lights to alert you to problems.

Heijunka: Level out the work load

Jidoka: Automation with the human touch

Takt Time: a German word for rhythm or meter. In lean, takt is the rate of customer demand. It's like a speedometer.

Poka-Yoke: mistake-proofing a process so that a person cannot make an error.

Kaikaku: radical or revolutionary improvement

Kaizen: continuous incremental improvement

Yes! I want Jay Arthur's fast, fun and easy-to-use Six Sigma Simplified System to work for me! *Please send the software and training material indicated.* (Offer good until 12/31/08)

☐ **QI Macros Starter Kit: (# 275)**
QI Macros (#230)
Training CD (#237)
Six Sigma Tools Book (#239)

Only $197   **Save $12**
*add $10 S&H, **add** $40 for FedEx*

☐ **SPC Simplified System: (#285)**
QI Macros (#230)
Training CD (#237)
Six Sigma Tools Book (#239)
SPC Simplified Book (#215)
SPC Simplified Video (#267)

Only $297   **Save $38**
*add $10 S&H, **add** $40 for FedEx*

☐ **Lean Six Sigma System: (#290/295)**
QI Macros #230 + Training CD #237
Lean Six Sigma books 205,210 215,239
Training Videos (#262, #265, #267)
5-Audio CDs (#225)   **Save $122**

☐ #290 Mfg   **Only $675**
☐ #295 Healthcare **Only $775**
includes Lean for Labs #263
*add $15 S&H, **add** $45 for FedEx*

Order Form

Qty.	Item		Price	FedEx	Mail	Total
	230	QI Macros for Excel (discounts for 2 or more)	$139	$25	$8	
	226	1-Year Maintenance and Upgrade Plan (4 qtrs + annual CD)	$60			
	227	2-year Maintenance and Upgrade Plan (8 qtrs + annual CDs)	$110			
	228	3-year Maintenance and Upgrade Plan (12 qtrs + annual CDs)	$160			
	237	QI Macros Training CD ROM	$49.95	$25	$6	
	239	Six Sigma Tools (Example Book)	$19.95	$25	$6	
	215	SPC Simplified book	$29.95	$25	$6	
	267	SPC Simplified Video (☐ Mfg ☐ Healthcare)	$97	$25	$10	
	262	Lean Simplified Video	$97	$25	$10	
	263	Lean for Healthcare Labs Video	$197	$25	$10	
	205	Six Sigma Simplified–Breakthrough Improvement Made Easy	$29.95	$25	$6	
Shipping and Handling:		**First individual item**				
U.S.		**Each additional Item: $2 (Mail) or $5 (FedEx)**				
					Order Total	

Please type or print clearly or attach business card here

Company _____

Your Name _____

Mailing Address _____

P.O. Box _____ Apt/Ste. _____

City, ST, Zip _____

Phone _____

Fax _____

Email _____

☐ Check here if you have ordered from us before

Yes! We also accept Purchase Orders!

Purchase Order Number _____
(to prevent duplicate shipments, <u>never</u> send confirming POs)

☐ VISA ☐ MasterCard ☐ AMEX
_____ Exp._____
Signature _____

☐ I've enclosed my check, VISA, MasterCard, or AmEx.

☐ I want to try them out **Absolutely Risk Free**. Please send my order immediately. *I have 30 days to pay the invoice or return them with no obligation.*

Order by 6/30/2008 to Receive these Special Bonuses

Special Bonus #1 - *Lean Quick Reference Card*
Special Bonus #2 - *Six Sigma Quick Reference Card*
Special Bonus #3 - *SPC Quick Reference Card*
Orders Only
(To minimize errors please order on-line or fax your order)

Order On-line at: **www.qimacros.com**

FAX your order toll-free to: **(888) 468-1536** or
(303) 753-9675

LifeStar, 2253 S. Oneida St. Ste D3 Denver, CO 80224

Orders-only, Call Toll-free: (888) 468-1535 or
(Please have your item # ready) (303) 757-2039

Questions about the QI Macros?
email: lifestar@rmi.net, knowwareman@qimacros.com
9 a.m. to 5 p.m. MST   **(888) 468-1537** or
(303) 756-9144

90 Day, Unconditional, No Risk, Money-back Guarantee